# *Unclaimed Riches*

# *Unclaimed Riches*

*Rod Parsley*

**Unclaimed Riches**

Copyright © 2016 by Rod Parsley
ISBN 978-1-935794-20-2

Published by:
Results Publishing
World Harvest Church
P.O. Box 100
Columbus, Ohio 43216-0100

Printed in the United States of America. All rights reserved under International Copyright Law. Contents and/or cover may not be reproduced in whole or in part in any form without the expressed written consent of the Publisher.

Unless otherwise noted, all Scripture quotations are from the Modern English Version of the Holy Bible. Copyright © 2014 by Military Bible Association. Used by permission. All rights reserved.

Scripture quotations marked Amplified are taken from THE AMPLIFIED BIBLE, EXPANDED EDITION Copyright © 1987 by The Zondervan Corporation and The Lockman Foundation. Used by permission. All rights reserved.

Scripture quotations marked NIV are taken from THE NIV REFERENCE BIBLE Copyright © 1990 by The Zondervan Corporation. Used by permission. All rights reserved.

Definitions taken from INTERNATIONAL STANDARD BIBLE ENCYCLOPEDIA, Copyright © 1995-1996 by Biblesoft. All rights reserved.

# CONTENTS

*Introduction: Unclaimed Riches* ............................................................ 1

1  A New Beginning ............................................................................ 9

2  I'm On My Way Out ......................................................................25

3  There Are Giants in the Land! ......................................................41

4  It's Time to Cross Over! ................................................................57

5  Building a Memorial ......................................................................73

6  Possessing the Land of Promise ....................................................81

7  Hidden Treasures ...........................................................................91

*Receiving Your Unclaimed Riches* ......................................................105

## *Introduction*

## *Unclaimed Riches*

Not long ago, a local news program ran a special segment entitled, "Missing Money." Naturally, my curiosity was piqued.

Every day for several weeks the news anchor reporting the story would list several individuals' names supplied by the state agency in charge of estates. These were people whom they were seeking to give money which had been left to them either by a deceased relative, an uncollected tax refund or a bank account where money had accumulated throughout the years.

Each time this broadcast aired, this same news anchor proudly announced how they had helped people the previous week to whom they were able to help acquire their unclaimed fortunes. You can only imagine the excitement of these individuals who had found something they thought was lost, or in many instances never realized they had to begin with.

This new realm of undiscovered wealth has also produced many upstart companies who assert their abilities to uncover lost riches. They make statements such as, "We want you to help claim your lost money!"

Let me assure you: I am not discounting any of these sources as a way of recovering or uncovering lost money. However, all of this talk of discovering new wealth caused me to wonder.

How many Christians really understand the biblical principles relating to their finances? I believe that if we truly grasped the revelation in the Word of God concerning our money, we would begin to walk out of the land of lack and into God's supernatural blessing!

## Introduction

In the Gospel of Mark, Jesus shared a powerful parable:

*He said, "The kingdom of God is like a man who scatters seed on the ground. He sleeps and rises night and day, and the seed sprouts and grows; he does not know how. For the earth bears fruit by itself: first the blade, then the head, then the full seed in the head. But when the grain is ripe, immediately he applies the sickle because the harvest has come"* (4:26-29).

There is a harvest waiting for you. In the heavenly pavilions of glory, with hands opened wide, the Lord has something for you. It is your *unclaimed riches*.

Through this book, I want to take you on a journey. You will follow the exodus of Israel through the land of Egypt. You will traverse the deserts of a dry and parched wilderness with them. You will arrive on the brink of the Jordan River and cross over its flooded banks only to come face to face with

Jericho. However, in the end you will see why you and they made such a dramatic journey.

God had promised the Israelites a land filled with provision and harvest. All they had to do was successfully navigate, by faith, to the other side.

The Israelites had to make the determination to change their slave mentality. No longer were they to be wanderers in the wilderness. Now they were to become conquerors in the land of Canaan.

They were God's chosen people. The Bible says, through the new covenant of Jesus' shed blood, we are His chosen people as well.

*"But you are a chosen race, a royal priesthood, a holy nation, a people for God's own possession, so that you may declare the goodness of Him who has called you out of darkness into His*

## Introduction

*marvelous light. In times past, you were not a people, but now you are the people of God. You had not received mercy, but now you have received mercy"* (1 Peter 2:9-10).

We have all of the rights and privileges of the covenant to go get our harvest. You and I are part of the final generation destined to experience the manifestation of Almighty God. We have been called to the kingdom for such a time as this!

Financial breakthrough is one of the last bastions of satanic resistance before the imminent return of Jesus. As heirs to the promise, God wants to open His great storehouse of wealth. Provision has already been made for us to receive His abundant blessing.

As you read this book, may you discover just how much our heavenly Father wants us to be prosperous, as He said:

## Unclaimed Riches

*"I will go before you and make the crooked places straight; I will break in pieces the gates of bronze and shatter the bars of iron. And I will give you the treasures of darkness and hidden riches of secret places so that you may know that I, the LORD, who calls you by your name, am the God of Israel"* (Isaiah 45:2-3).

May you come to know that the Lord wants His people to be prosperous. He wants *you* to be prosperous.

These are our final days, and the best is yet to come. There is a great transfer of wealth about to take place, and the Lord wants to reveal to you that your harvest is already waiting.

There is a harvest of salvation, healing, deliverance and financial blessing waiting for you on the other side of Jordan. God has given you the anointing and the ability to reap.

## Introduction

It is time to claim what rightfully belongs to you. It is time to go get your *unclaimed riches*.

# One

## *A New Beginning*

There is something special about a new beginning. When a person receives a pardon, either from a governor or the President of the United States, something unique takes place. Not only does the individual who received the pardon get released from jail, but there also no longer exists a record of his or her alleged wrong doing. It is as though their past has been wiped clean.

We are living in the beginning of a new millennium. It is a time when, as 2 Corinthians 5:17 says:

> *"Therefore, if any man is in Christ, he is a new creature. Old things have passed away. Look, all things have become new."*

We are living in the final days when all things become new again!

Did you know that what is happening *in* you is greater than what is happening *to* you? I believe that in the days to come, in this new millennium you will not recognize yourself, your family or any area of your life. God is about to do a brand new thing. The former things will pass away. Your old way of doing things is about to die so that God can resurrect it anew. Your lack mentality is about to pass away so that the Lord can instill in your spirit mountain moving faith in every area of your life according to Mark 11:22-24:

*"Jesus answered them, "Have faith in God. For truly I say to you, whoever says to this mountain, 'Be removed and be thrown into the sea,' and does not doubt in his heart, but believes that what he says will come to pass, he will have whatever he says. Therefore I say to you, whatever things you ask when you pray, believe that you will receive them, and you will have them."*

## A New Beginning

How is He going to do it? Ephesians 3:20 says:

*"Now to Him who is able to do exceedingly abundantly beyond all that we ask or imagine, according to the power that works in us..."*

God is able to save you from a life marked by lack. The Lord is about to deliver you from the chains of debt. God is able to set you free from a poverty mindset. God is able to place within you a new heart and a new spirit that is full of faith to believe for anything that you need.

Ezekiel 36:26-30 declares:

*"Also, I will give you a new heart, and a new spirit I will put within you. And I will take away the stony heart out of your flesh, and I will give you a heart of flesh. I will put My Spirit within you and cause you to walk in My statutes, and you will keep My judgments and do them. You will dwell in the land that I gave to your fathers. And you will be My people, and I will be your God. I will also save you from all your uncleanness. And I*

*will call for the grain and increase it and lay no famine upon you. I will multiply the fruit of the tree and the increase of the field so that you shall receive no more reproach of famine among the nations."*

Do you remember when you were first saved? Everything seemed brighter. Everyone seemed happier. Your body felt better and it was as if nothing would ever go wrong.

I believe the Lord is about to put a new anointing on you so that it will be like you were just first saved. You will be like one who dreams a dream and won't want to wake up because the blessing of God will be so rich upon your life.

Psalm 126:1 says:

*"When the LORD restored the captives of Zion, we were like those who dream."*

## A New Thing

God gave me a very specific word which was declared by the prophet, Isaiah:

*"Thus says the LORD, who makes a way in the sea and a path in the mighty waters, who brings forth the chariot and horse, the army and the mighty men (they shall lie down together, they shall not rise; they are extinguished, they are quenched like a wick): Do not remember the former things nor consider the things of old. See, I will do a new thing, now it shall spring forth; shall you not be aware of it? I will even make a way in the wilderness, and rivers in the desert"* (43:16-19).

In verses 16 and 17 of this passage of scripture, the Lord reminded Israel of the mighty things He did for their fathers when He brought them out of the land of Egypt.

In order to build upon our faith, it is important for us to remember what God did for us in the past. The Psalmist declared:

*"Bless the LORD, O my soul, and forget not all His benefits, who forgives all your iniquities, who heals all your diseases, who redeems your life from the pit, who crowns you with lovingkindness and tender mercies, who satisfies your mouth with good things, so that your youth is renewed like the eagle's"* (103:2-5).

Jehovah Nissi, the Lord our banner of victory, does not want us to forget the victories He has wrought on our behalf. However, He has new victories and fresh mercies awaiting us in the land of harvest.

Lamentations 3:22-23 states:

*"It is of the LORD's mercies that we are not consumed; His compassions do not fail. They are new every morning; great is Your faithfulness."*

## A New Beginning

Jehovah had wrought a wonderful work by causing the Israelites to pass through the Red Sea as they fled their taskmasters' bondage. What became a passage for them became a barrier for the Egyptians. The Red Sea became a source of safety to the Israelites while it became a stumbling block to their enemies. The water became a refuge and a road for God's chosen people.

The way to Canaan was through a dry, parched desert land. The same God who made a way in the sea can make a way in the wilderness. He that made dry land of the Red Sea can and will make dry land of the Jordan River.

God made a way where there was no way. I like to say it this way. Where there is a will – a "want to," an expectation – there is a way!

So many times our miracle is dependent upon knowing the will of our heavenly Father. Jesus left us His last will and testament through His inspired Word, our very own Bible.

However, so many times we do not take the time to find out what the will of God is for our lives. Jesus admonished:

*"You search the Scriptures, because you think in them you have eternal life. These are they who bear witness of Me"* (John 5:39).

In order to perpetuate the will of God in our family, health and finances, we must ask Him for whatever we need.

1 John 5:14 states:

*"This is the confidence that we have in Him, that if we ask anything according to His will, He hears us."*

I believe many misinterpret this verse to mean that if we ask anything according to God's will, only then will He hear us. However, I believe in actuality what the Holy Spirit is saying is that if we ask anything it is God's will to hear and answer us.

## *A New Beginning*

How many prayers have been prayed like this: "If it be thy will, help me get out of debt. If it be thy will, help me to have more than enough to meet my needs."

I have good Gospel news for you! When we find out the will of God, according to His Word, then we will understand that He desires for us to prosper.

*"Beloved, I pray that all may go well with you and that you may be in good health, even as your soul is well"* (3 John 2).

### NOW SHALL THEY SPRING FORTH

I want you to notice one last point in Isaiah 43:19:

*"See, I will do a new thing, now it shall spring forth; shall you not be aware of it? I will even make a way in the wilderness, and rivers in the desert."*

The new thing God is about to do shall spring forth now. You do not have to wait for our unclaimed riches any longer.

Your harvest is already in the field waiting for you just to put the sickle in and reap.

So many Christians are still waiting on their harvest. They have waited and waited, believing that someday it will happen. The time is now and this is the day!

## THIRD DAY CHRISTIANS

The time to be passive is over. This is a time of passing over and possessing your promised harvest in every area of your life! You have not passed this way before!

This is the year when you are on your way out of the wilderness and into the land of Canaan to reap your promised harvest.

For years, it seemed, we were on the brink of Jordan's banks. We had not been able to cross to the other side to possess our promised harvest.

## *A New Beginning*

However, as we moved into the 21st century, I believe the Lord showed me through the prophet Hosea that we have just now entered the third day.

*"Come, let us return to the LORD, for He has torn, and He will heal us. He has struck, and He will bind us up. After two days He will revive us. On the third day He will raise us up, that we may live before Him. Let us know, let us press on to know the LORD. His appearance is as sure as the dawn. He will come to us like the rain; like the spring rains He will water the earth"* (6:1-3).

We are living in the third day when old things pass away and all things become new!

The third day represents resurrection day. It was the third day when Jesus kicked the end out of a borrowed tomb and rose again as our Savior and Canaan King.

It was three days that Joshua was told to wait and prepare before crossing the Jordan River.

## *Unclaimed Riches*

We are getting ready to bury our past and resurrect a new beginning in every area of our lives. We are living in a time where wanderers become conquerors.

You are not just going to conquer your unclaimed riches in your life. You are going to reap your harvest in your family as well.

It is a new day for a new church, full of new believers, with a new song, with a new shout, with a new word.

God is about to push you over the edge into your harvest. It's time to get up. It's time to go. It's time to go get what belongs to us.

### JUST DO IT!

What is the first step to reaping your harvest? The answer is found in the Gospel of John and Jesus' first miracle at the wedding of Cana.

The Bible records these words:

## A New Beginning

> *On the third day there was a wedding in Cana of Galilee. The mother of Jesus was there. Both Jesus and His disciples were invited to the wedding. When the wine ran out, the mother of Jesus said to Him, "They have no wine." Jesus said to her, "Woman, what does this have to do with Me? My hour has not yet come." His mother said to the servants, "Whatever He says to you, do it"* (John 2:1-5).

Jesus told the servants to fill the water pots with water, and then He turned the water into wine.

What was the significance of Jesus' word to the servants? How did His Word compare to the obedience of Naaman, the leper, dipping seven times in the Jordan River? Nothing, except that both Jesus and the prophet, Elisha, said to do it!

The first step to reaping your harvest is, whatsoever the Holy Spirit is saying unto you, do it!

## Jesus Is Looking for You!

Jesus is looking for some third day Christians who are ready to march forward and possess their unclaimed riches! Make no mistake about it – God will have a day. He will have an hour. God will have a moment when His church, full of His power, will stand in complete authority upon the face of this earth.

My question to you is, Why not you? Why not here? Why not now?

You see, we don't need everybody. Just as on the day of Pentecost when 120 believers gathered together in the Upper Room, give me a band of believers who, possessed by the Holy Spirit, hate nothing but sin and love nothing but God.

I don't care whether they are preachers, clergy or laity, for these and these alone will storm hell's brazen gates and lift up their hands and declare:

## A New Beginning

*"Your kingdom come; Your will be done on earth, as it is in heaven"* (Matthew 6:10).

I believe as you read the remaining chapters of this book you are about to go where you have never been. Deep within my spirit I believe you are about to give birth to a miracle you didn't even know you were carrying.

There is a harvest waiting for you on the other side of Jordan's banks. However, first you must prepare to leave the wilderness. Get ready to declare: I am on my way out!

## Two

## *I'm On My Way Out*

Joshua gathered the children of Israel together on the anniversary of the dividing of the Red Sea. It was hard to imagine that forty years had passed since Moses led the children of Israel out of Egyptian bondage. The last generation had passed with the death of Moses, and now a new generation had emerged.

Positioned on the brink of the Jordan River, with the wilderness behind them and the promised land before them, Joshua gave the children of Israel their marching orders to pass over:

> *Then Joshua commanded the officers of the people, "Pass through the midst of the camp and command the people, 'Prepare food, for in three days you will cross the Jordan to go to take pos-*

*session of the land that the* LORD *your God is giving you to possess*' " (vv. 10-11).

On the muddy banks of Jordan, Joshua told the people to get ready.

There were three things the Lord told the children of Israel to do. First, they were to prepare victuals.

Their leadership had changed. Their source of direction – the cloud by day and the pillar of fire by night – was all but a memory.

Manna was the staple of their wilderness food. However, their supply of manna and quail would cease in three days. The Lord told them to prepare to cross Jordan's stormy banks in three days.

How often God commands us to set aside that thing to which we have become accustomed. The Israelites were used to their daily provision of manna. Fear told them to hold onto the past. Faith told them to cross over to the promise.

## TO COME OUT, YOU MUST FIRST GO IN

In order for Joshua and the children of Israel to enter into the promised land they must first come out. In order to get where they were going they had to make the determination to leave where they were.

Deuteronomy 26:1 says:

*"And it must be, when you come into the land which the LORD your God is giving you for an inheritance, and you possess it, and dwell in it..."*

The first thing that God said in this verse is *when you come in*. Life is the process of exchange. For instance, in order for you to breathe in, God must first breathe out. You sit down only that you may stand up. You must leave one room to enter another room. In order to enter Canaan, the Israelites must first leave the wilderness.

## Unclaimed Riches

In order to get where you are going you have to make the determination to leave where you are.

The kingdom of God is diametrically opposed to the kingdom of darkness. What does this mean?

So many have just determined that they can't get out of their situation. They say they are living in the promised land, but they look like they are still wearing Egyptian slave clothes. They have a slave mentality.

Colossians 1:12-13 says:

*"...giving thanks to the Father, who has enabled us to be partakers in the inheritance of the saints in light. He has delivered us from the power of darkness and has transferred us into the kingdom of His dear Son..."*

I was in Germany several years ago, and I had the unique opportunity to travel on the Autobahn. This was a stretch of highway where there was no speed limit. At the time I did not know this, and though it seemed like we were driving fast, we were still being passed by other motorists.

I asked the gentleman who was driving, "What is the speed limit? Either we are going too slow or everyone else is breaking the law." He replied, "There is no speed limit on the Autobahn. You can drive as fast as you want to." My immediate response was to tell him to see what our car could do!

It is time to take the limits off of God. He has given us a kingdom where we don't have to beg and plead to receive our unclaimed riches. All we have to do is reap.

## CHANGE YOUR MIND ABOUT YOUR HARVEST

However, in order to do this we need to repent of our poverty thinking. Matthew 4:17 says:

> *From that time Jesus began to preach, saying, "Repent! For the kingdom of heaven is at hand."*

## Unclaimed Riches

The first thing Jesus commands us to do is to repent. Repentance means to change your mind about God and toward God. For many years, the body of Christ has been indoctrinated with the theology that we must be poor. However, God says, "Change your mind to my way of doing things."

God's ways are not our ways. Isaiah 55 says it this way:

*"For My thoughts are not your thoughts, nor are your ways My ways, says the LORD. For as the heavens are higher than the earth, so are My ways higher than your ways, and My thoughts than your thoughts"* (vv. 8-9).

The Lord has delivered us so that we might receive our unclaimed riches in Christ Jesus. Therefore, we need to lay aside a slave mentality. We should no longer settle for the crumbs that fall off of the table. There's a chair at the King's table with your name on it, and it is time to take your rightful place. We must leave where we've been on the way to where we are going.

*I'm On My Way Out*

The second thing Jesus says in Matthew 4:17 is that the kingdom of heaven is at hand. God's heavenly order is established on earth. What is that order? We have enthroned the exiled King in our life and we must give Him the preeminence. Therefore, we live in a theocracy, not a democracy. What the Bible says is our rule of conduct. If the Bible says we are to live abundantly, then that should be our code of conduct.

The last thing Jesus said in this passage of Scripture was that His kingdom was at hand. It wasn't coming years later, it was already here! Why? Because Jesus had already arrived, and where He is, every provision He has already made is ours now.

We must make the decision to leave the land of low living, sight walking, mundane dreams, tame vision, smooth knees, distress, discouragement, death, disease, and poverty. We are on our way out! We are going to change our address!

*Unclaimed Riches*

The land that we are going into is unlike the land that we are leaving. That land was a place where we could take the sole of our foot and carve out places for the water to run.

The land God is leading us into is a land of hills and valleys. It is a place where we must put our total trust in Jehovah God. Why?

Because we can't come out of bondage and into the land of plenty on our own. However, God is about to open the windows of heaven that will lead us into a land of supernatural harvest.

You need to let go of what you have held on to in the past. For example, your job is only a method God uses to get you where you need to be for the opportunity of kingdom advancement.

Are you satisfied with your life? Let your only satisfaction be your dissatisfaction be with where you are.

## RENEWING YOUR MIND

God has always delivered with a seed. You can shout, "I'm on my way out" all day, but until you make the determination to refuse to stay like you have been, in bondage to debt and lack, you will never enter in the promised land and reap your promised harvest.

The first thing you have to do is renew your mind and make the determination that you are coming out of the wilderness.

Romans 12:1-2 states:

*"I urge you therefore, brothers, by the mercies of God, that you present your bodies as a living sacrifice, holy, and acceptable to God, which is your reasonable service of worship. Do not be conformed to this world, but be transformed by the renewing of your mind, that you may prove what is the good and acceptable and perfect will of God."*

*Unclaimed Riches*

In order to know the will of God, we must have a mind that is renewed in the Word, a will that is submitted to that Word and emotions that are controlled, not controlling.

Faith begins where the will of God is known. Unless you are assured of the will of God, there is no foundation for faith. Without faith, you and I are just hoping that what we believe may come to pass.

We are like the man described in James 1:

*"But let him ask in faith, without wavering. For he who wavers is like a wave of the sea, driven and tossed with the wind. Let not that man think that he will receive anything from the Lord. A double-minded man is unstable in all his ways"* (vv. 6-8).

A double minded man is not a confused man, but he is an undecided man. His spirit says one thing, but because he has not renewed himself in the Word of God, his mind tells him something completely different.

*I'm On My Way Out*

God's Word and the Spirit always agree. Therefore, God's Word is the final authority on any matter in your life. If the Bible says God wants you to be prosperous, your family to be saved or your body to be healed then that is God's will for you. There is no other option.

Hebrews 11:6 states:

*"And without faith it is impossible to please God, for he who comes to God must believe that He exists and that He is a rewarder of those who diligently seek Him."*

Perfect faith cannot exist where the will of God is not known. Therefore, once I know God's will I have ahold of something called absolute truth. If I grasp hold of absolute truth, it doesn't matter to me what anyone has to say. If I hang on to truth, then nothing can turn my plow.

With the truth of God's Word, I can stand next door to hell, raise my hands and believe that whatsoever God has promised He is able also to perform!

## *Unclaimed Riches*

I don't know what it takes to get your faith activated. But you need to do something you have never done before. You need to step out into a different dimension than you've experienced up to now. God is declaring an outpouring of abundant harvest.

The devil can't talk you out of your blessing, because you have looked across Jordan's flooding banks and have seen your harvest. It is waiting for you. It is your time for your thing from your God.

### YOU ARE ON YOUR WAY OUT!

This is no time to look back to your past. This is no time to hope for a prolonged present.

Now is the time to look over your left shoulder. Turn back around and look over your right shoulder, and decide that is the last time you look back.

## I'm On My Way Out

It is time to make this declaration of faith: "I am on my way out and into my promised harvest!"

There isn't anything back there in the land of Egypt for you but captivity and chains. You are going to another level! You're going to another level in your praise! You're going to another level in your shout!

I believe there are many in the body of Christ who are tired of being where they have been – under the table looking for crumbs – when God wants to give them His kingdom!

The Gospel of Luke says:

*"Do not be afraid, little flock, for it is your Father's good pleasure to give you the kingdom"* (12:32).

You can't stay in the land of bondage. You are on your way out. I believe you are tired of wearing shoes that don't wear out. You are tired of eating manna pancakes in the morning and manna burgers at night. You are coming out of debt, depravity and disease! You can't stay here any longer!

## Unclaimed Riches

Aren't you tired of where you've been?

Make this confession of faith: "I can't wear those chains of lack any longer. I'm on my way out. I can't be discouraged by debt. I'm on my way out! I can't wear the shackles labeled not enough. I'm on my way out!"

Did you know that you can't stop a man whose already seen his harvest on the other side of Jordan? I have seen too much to stay where I am right now! I am on my way out! You can't block me. I'm on my way out! You can't stop me. I'm on my way out!

We are part of the remnant people who will not be denied their position, delayed in their pursuit or detoured on the pathway to their promise. Why? Because we are on our way out!

Many believers have taken another route to their harvest. However, God is about to make a highway for you through the wilderness.

## *I'm On My Way Out*

Don't you back up. Maybe you have hit a little bump in the road of hard times. Someone may have given you a bad report. Perhaps things don't look good at the bottom of your checkbook balance. That's not a time to quit. That's a time to man your battle stations, ready your weapons, lock and load. There is a Holy Ghost revolution about to take place in your life.

What are you believing for today?

I stand in covenant agreement with my partners and friends, and we declare into the spirit realm that our harvest is already on the way. We believe our words pierce the heavenlies and that the anointing upon them destroys every yoke of bondage, barrier and burden of debt and lack, in Jesus' name!

It doesn't matter what the report may look like – God said He would bless us coming in and bless us going out! We are on our way out, and victory is assured!

1 Corinthians 2:9 proclaims:

## Unclaimed Riches

*But as it is written, "Eye has not seen, nor ear heard, nor has it entered into the heart of man the things which God has prepared for those who love Him."*

There is a harvest waiting just on the other side of Jordan. The grapes are ripe and the land is plentiful. Don't allow the devil to keep you from your greatest breakthrough!

Make the determination today. Draw a line in the sand and say, "I may not be out, but I'm on my way out. I am going to start in the right direction."

Make the decision to cross this Jordan and inherit everything that God has in store for you.

## *Three*

# *There Are Giants in the Land*

Many Christians do not understand why they do not reap their unclaimed riches. Two of the greatest tools the devil will use against you to keep you wandering in the wilderness are fear and greed.

These were two obstacles that kept the first generation of Israelites from entering into the promised land.

### OVERCOMING THE SPIRIT OF FEAR

What generates fear? False evidence appearing real.

Luke 21:26 proclaims:

*"...men fainting from fear and expectation of what is coming on the inhabited earth. For the powers of heaven will be shaken."*

What will men and women fear? They will fear anything – fear of the economy, fear of failure, fear of financial crisis. The devil would like nothing more than to grip your heart with fear and paralyze you so that you are unable to fulfill the call of God upon your life.

Ecclesiastes 11:4 says:

*"He who observes the wind will not sow, and he who regards the clouds will not reap."*

Let me share this with you: the greatest satanic opposition always comes right before your greatest breakthrough!

Here's an example: Before Moses died and Joshua arose in leadership, and before entering the promised land, the land flowing with milk and honey, Moses sent twelve spies to spy out the land.

Ten of them would return with an evil report. However, two of them, Joshua and Caleb, would return with a proclamation of promise and blessing. Numbers 14:7-10 declares:

## There Are Giants in the Land

> *"And they spoke to all the assembly of the children of Israel, saying, "The land which we passed through to explore it is a very, very good land. If the LORD delights in us, then He will bring us into this land and give it to us, a land which flows with milk and honey. Only do not rebel against the LORD, nor fear the people of the land because they are bread for us. Their defense is gone from them, and the LORD is with us. Do not fear them."*

Unfortunately, the popular opinion was to stay back in the land of just enough – the land of living day to day – the land of mediocrity – all because of fear.

Fear is the opposite of faith, and it will paralyze the operation of the blessing of God in your life.

If the children of Israel would have only remembered that Joshua wanted to take them into the promised land, then they wouldn't have been paralyzed by fear.

## Unclaimed Riches

Provision prophesies provision. Supply is a prophetic indication of future supply. Victory in the past is a prophetic indicator of victory in the future.

Unfortunately, many Christians are living in what I like to call the someday syndrome. They think, "Well, someday I will have more than enough. Someday I will be healed, and someday I will walk in the blessing of God."

"Someday," my friend, never comes. The Bible says:

*"In an acceptable time I have listened to you, and in the day of salvation I have helped you"* (2 Corinthians 6:2).

Let me make this announcement. The fearful cannot strike any heavy blow in the hour of conflict. Fear paralyzes the arm because it unnerves the heart. However, men who are possessed by the Holy Spirit do not seek deliverance from the fires of adversity, nor do they petition the courts of heaven for tasks equal to their powers. Rather, they plead upon their knees for power that is equal to their task.

Today, you need to make the decision to proclaim, "Today, I enter the land. Today, the promise is mine. Today, I have more than enough! "I refuse to ever be comfortable with lack again; lack of resources; lack of health; lack of freedom in my spirit!"

## **WITHHOLDING GOD'S PORTION**

The second reason people do not sow seed is greed, or, in other words, withholding for your own use that which belongs to God. Proverbs 3: 9-10 proclaims:

*"Honor the LORD with your substance, and with the first fruits of all your increase; so your barns will be filled with plenty, and your presses will burst out with new wine."*

When you do this an amazing thing happens, and Romans 11:16 declares:

*"If the first portion of the dough is holy, the batch is also holy. And if the root is holy, so are the branches."*

## Unclaimed Riches

What is God saying? He is saying sanctify or set apart your finances unto Him. If you will sanctify your firstfruits unto Him, the whole will be sanctified, and the whole is everything that pertains to you! Everything in your life is to be set apart unto Him.

If you earn $100 and bring a crisp, new $10 bill to the Lord as His tithe, it is not an ordinary piece of currency any more than the rod of Moses was an ordinary stick or the mantle of Elijah was an ordinary piece of cloth. Your tithe has already been earmarked by the Lord – as if He folded the corner down and said, "This one is mine." Therefore, it has miracle-working power.

When God touches that little piece of paper in your hand, He can multiply it until a mountain of obligations disappear. Stretch forth your seed over the distress of your life and watch your miracle begin. The Lord will part the waters of debt and distress and you will walk on dry ground.

## THE BATTLE OF AI

For all of Joshua's great accomplishments – 31 campaigns in all – there was one time in which the disobedience of one brought a reproach and, ultimately, defeat to the children of Israel. It was at the battle of Ai.

*Yet the children of Israel violated their obligations with regard to the things dedicated for destruction. Achan, son of Karmi, son of Zimri, son of Zerah, from the tribe of Judah took from the things dedicated for destruction, and the anger of the LORD burned against the children of Israel. Joshua sent men from Jericho to Ai (which is near Beth Aven, east of Bethel) and said to them, "Go up and spy on the land." So the men went up and spied on Ai.*

*Then they returned to Joshua and said to him, "All the people need not go up. Let about two or three thousand men go up and strike Ai. Since they are so few, all the people need not weary themselves." So about three thousand men went up from among the people there, but they fled from before the men of Ai. The men of Ai struck down thirty-six men and pursued them from the gate to Shebarim. They struck them down on the mountainside, and the hearts of the people melted like water.*

*Israel has sinned, and they have broken My covenant that I commanded them. They took from the things dedicated for destruction. They have stolen, acted deceitfully, and put them among their own possessions. Therefore the children of Israel cannot stand before their enemies. They turn their backs to their enemies because they have become dedicated for destruction. I will not be with you anymore if you do not destroy the things dedicated for destruction in your midst* (Joshua 7:1-5,11,12).

There were several reasons why Israel lost the battle at Ai. First, they were affected by the disobedience of one, namely Achan. Psalm 133:1 says, "Behold, how good and how pleasant it is for brethren to dwell together in unity."

Second, they committed a national sin. Malachi 3:9 states:

*"You are cursed with a curse, your whole nation, for you are robbing Me."*

Third, everyone did not go to battle. Verse three said that the spies persuaded Joshua to let only a few go to fight.

You must never underestimate the power of your adversary. There is no time to relax or take your enemy for granted. The Bible commands us:

*"Be sober and watchful, because your adversary the devil walks around as a roaring lion, seeking whom he may devour"* (1 Peter 5:8).

The last thing Joshua failed to do was to properly communicate the vision of God. Habakkuk 2:2 says:

*"And the Lord answered me: Write the vision, and make it plain on tablets, that he who reads it may run."*

When the vision, plan and purpose of God are properly communicated, there is provision, protection and supply.

However, the flesh will always war against the spirit, regardless of how noble the cause.

Galatians 4:29 states:

*"But as it was then, he who was born after the flesh persecuted him who was born after the Spirit, so it is now also."*

In our day and age, all the people are to share the responsibility of the church. We are to depend on God, not on a human or human strength.

Our tithing, or lack thereof, affects the corporate body. 1 Corinthians 12 proclaims:

*For as the body is one and has many parts, and all the many parts of that one body are one body, so also is Christ. For by one Spirit we are all baptized into one body, whether we are Jews or Gentiles, whether we are slaves or free, and we have all been made to drink of one Spirit. The body is not one part, but many. And if the ear says, "Because I am not the eye, I am not of the body," is it therefore not of the body?"* (vv. 12-14,16)

Do not allow the devil to deceive you. You are important to the body of Christ. Your time, talent and treasure are integral to the purpose God has for His body – to ultimately bring lost souls into His kingdom.

## THE GOLDEN GOBLETS

Another example of using that which is sanctified unto the Lord is found in the book of Daniel.

*"...but have lifted up yourself against the Lord of heaven. And they have brought the vessels of His house before you, and you and your lords, your wives and your concubines, have drunk wine in them. And you have praised the gods of silver and gold, of bronze, iron, wood, and stone, which see not, nor hear, nor know. And the God in whose hand is your breath, and whose*

*are all your ways, you have not glorified. Then the hand was sent from Him, and this inscription was written.*

*"This is the inscription that was written: MENE, MENE, TEKEL, UPHARSIN. This is the interpretation of the message: MENE: God has numbered your kingdom and put an end to it. TEKEL: you have been weighed in the balances and are found wanting"* (5:23-27).

Belshazzar used the golden goblets, sanctified to God, for a profane use. Therefore, he was weighed in the balance and found wanting.

His enemies invaded the land because he opened the door to the devil. Then the river dried up.

In our day, the river is symbolic of the Holy Spirit. When disobedience is present, the move of God in our life is quenched. Then we lack provision or supply.

The end result in Belshazzar's case was that he died. How often have we allowed our harvest to die on the vine or rot in the field because of our disobedience to change our mind and to be obedient in every area of our lives.

## OBEDIENCE IS BETTER THAN SACRIFICE

Israel's first king, Saul, is yet another illustration of how greed can cause judgment to come upon a people.

> *And Saul said to Samuel, "I have obeyed the voice of the LORD. And I have followed in the way which the LORD sent me, and have brought Agag the king of Amalek, and have utterly destroyed the Amalekites. But the people took from the plunder sheep and oxen, the first fruits of the banned things to sacrifice to the LORD your God in Gilgal. Samuel said, "Does the LORD delight in burnt offerings and sacrifices as much as in obeying the voice of the LORD? Obedience is better than sacrifice, a listening ear than the fat of rams"* (1 Samuel 15:20-22).

There were several ways in which Saul was disobedient. He did not destroy the spoils of war. He disobeyed the voice of the prophet. The end result was that his kingdom was taken from him.

Disobedience can cause the blessing to be forfeited. It also opens the door for the devil. Lastly, it can cut off your source of help.

We can choose, through an act of obedience, to sanctify the Lord on the inside of us. As we do so, our seed is sanctified.

Therefore, we must make the determination not to use it for anything but that for which it was intended to be used.

We are kingdom people who don't need position or popularity. We don't need a pat on the back. We don't cave in when the going gets rough. We are happy to be in the battle. We are kingdom people who are tired of status quo Christianity. We are tired of not having enough to make ends meet. We are tired of sickness in our bodies.

## *There Are Giants in the Land*

Like an army with banners we are crossing Jordan to possess the land. We will stand with our feet firmly planted in our promised land and proclaim a genuine, culture-shaking financial revolution is underway. We are taking this kingdom by force!

## *Four*

## *It's Time to Cross Over*

For three days the children of Israel had prepared themselves to cross over the Jordan River. These remnant people were not like their forefathers who, because of doubt, fear and greed could not enter in.

What a sobering thought! How we must protect ourselves from the snares of the adversary when Canaan is waiting on just the other side!

Let's look again at Joshua 1:10-11:

*Then Joshua commanded the officers of the people, "Pass through the midst of the camp and command the people, 'Prepare food, for in three days you will cross the Jordan to go to take possession of the land that the LORD your God is giving you to possess.' "*

It was time to pass over the Jordan into their promised possession. They were not called to linger on the brink, not to sit with their feet in the water. They were commanded to pass over. They were about to put an end to their wilderness wanderings.

Let me interject this here: let not your heart be troubled! God knows how to take you through the river. The prophet Isaiah declared:

*"Was it not You who dried up the sea, the waters of the great deep, who made the depths of the sea a pathway for the ransomed to pass over? Therefore, the redeemed of the LORD shall return and come with singing to Zion, and everlasting joy shall be upon their head. They shall obtain gladness and joy, and sorrow and mourning shall flee away"* (51:10-11).

It is ours to submit to the command of our Canaan King. It is God's prerogative to prepare the way.

## **THE BREAKER GOES BEFORE US**

How were the Israelites to pass over the Jordan River? They saw no visible way to navigate to the other side. No bridge, road or boat existed. However, they were commanded to follow the ark of the Lord according to Joshua 3:11:

*"See, the ark of the covenant of the LORD of all the earth is passing before you into the Jordan."*

Let me interject this thought: the wind of the Holy Ghost is about to blow. God will blow all the props out from under you, and God will get rid of everything that you've depended on. Because He refuses to allow you to depend on anything but Him.

Let not your heart be troubled. God will make a way through the waters.

Micah 2:13 states:

## Unclaimed Riches

> *"He who breaks through has gone up before them; they will break through and pass the gate and go out by it. Then their king will pass on before them, the LORD at their head."*

Our Breaker, Jesus Christ, is gone before us. He alone knows how to take you through.

At times we vainly attempt to provide our own harvest and neglect to obey the Word of the Lord. Jehovah will make a way, if we will but take Him at His Word.

When hopelessness is knocking at your door, when defeat seems sure, know that your breakthrough is just across the river. When the night seems the longest, know that the dawn is about to break.

The first part of Song of Solomon 6:10 declares:

> *"Who is this who looks forth like the dawn, fair as the moon, radiant as the sun, awesome as an army with banners?"*

This is a picture of the modern church. This is the image of the Holy Ghost filled, fire- baptized, remnant church of Jesus Christ. This is the portrait of a people who are possessed with the spirit of the Breaker. They rise up, for they understand that their power and strength comes from God alone.

It doesn't matter how sultry or sullen the night has been. It doesn't matter that you may not be able to see across the river's banks. When the sun begins to break on the meridian horizon, you will begin to see your unclaimed riches on the other side!

## I WILL DRIVE OUT THE ENEMY

This generation was fearless and courageous. Though Jericho waited on the other side, with its walled city and formidable army, God has given the children of Israel another word:

*"And Joshua said, 'By this you will know that the living God is among you, and that He will thoroughly drive out the*

*Canaanites, the Hittites, the Hivites, the Perizzites, the Girgashites, the Amorites, and the Jebusites from before you"* (Joshua 3:10).

What will the Lord do? He will without fail drive out the inhabitants of the land. In other words, God will deliver you from all sin, sickness, disease, depravity, debt and poverty.

This word was further confirmed when Joshua sent men to spy out Jericho.

*"Then Joshua son of Nun sent two men out from Shittim to spy, saying, "Go see the land, especially Jericho." So they went, and they came to the house of a prostitute named Rahab. They spent the night there. She said to the men, "I know that the LORD has given you the land, for dread from you has fallen upon us, and all the inhabitants of the land melt in terror before you. For we heard how the LORD dried up the waters of the Red Sea before you when you came out of Egypt, and what you did to Sihon and Og, the two kings of the Amorites who were on the other*

*side of the Jordan, whom you completely destroyed. Our hearts melted when we heard these things, and no man had any breath in him because of you, for the LORD your God is God in heaven above and on earth below"* (Joshua 2:1, 9-11).

The hearts of the people of Jericho fainted within them because of all that the Lord had done on behalf of the children of Israel. Rahab confirmed that Jericho would be given into their hands.

Unlike Moses who sent twelve spies into the land, Joshua only sent two. These men had the spirit of the Breaker on the inside of them, and they delivered a different message to their leader.

*They said to Joshua, "The LORD has surely given the whole land into our hands! Indeed, all the inhabitants of the land melt in terror before us"* (v. 24).

## Unclaimed Riches

When the Lord drives out the enemy, the spoils always belong to the victor. There are unclaimed riches waiting for you on the other side of Jordan.

Philippians 4:19 says:

*"But my God shall supply your every need according to His riches in glory by Christ Jesus."*

The atmosphere of expectancy is the breeding ground of miracles. This is no time to hesitate or back up!

### WHAT ARE YOU PURSUING?

The proof of desire is in pursuit. For too long the church has been satisfied with where they are and what they have. The adversary has been successful at deceiving them that there could not possibly be any more blessing, healing or deliverance waiting for them. "After all," the devil whispers in the ears of some, "miracles and blessing ceased to exist when the last apostle died."

Somewhere, however, there have been those, a remnant, who have caught a glimpse of the other side of Jordan. Like Joshua and Caleb, they have seen the giants, but they have also seen the provision!

Let me repeat: the proof of desire is in pursuit! God has already promised you every good thing in His kingdom. Jeremiah 29:11 says:

*"For I know the thought and plans that I have for you, says the Lord, thoughts and plans for welfare and peace and not for evil, to give you hope in your final outcome"* (Amplified).

However, ask yourself this question, "What am I pursuing?"

Several years ago an evangelist friend of mine came to our church to minister. He was very gifted and anointed as a musician as well. He has written several familiar songs which have been a blessing to the body of Christ for many years. It was not uncommon for him to sit at a piano and begin to sing unto the Lord beautiful anointed psalms.

After one service I said to this man, "I wish I could play the piano like you." His response was, "No you don't." I was taken aback. "Yes I do. I wish I could sit at the piano and play before the Lord like you." His response again was, "No, you don't. How many piano lessons have you taken? What are you doing to increase your ability to play the piano?"

It was then that I understood what he was saying. If I truly wanted to learn to play the piano like him, I would pursue every avenue to increase my abilities to play.

It is the same in our finances or any area of our lives. If we truly wanted to be out of debt or financial lack – if we really wanted to be delivered or healed – we would begin to devour the Word of God and seek after Him with our whole heart.

The Psalmist proclaimed:

> *"This is Jacob, the generation of those who seek Him, who seek Your face. Selah"* (24:6).

Like Joshua's generation, I believe we are those who desire a true relationship with the Lord. As we do, Matthew 6:33 promises:

> *"But seek first the kingdom of God and His righteousness, and all these things shall be given to you."*

## IT'S TIME TO GO!

Three days had passed and it was time for the Israelites to leave the land of wandering. Joel 2:1 declares:

> *"Blow the ram's horn in Zion, sound the alarm on My holy mountain! All the inhabitants of the earth will tremble, because the day of the LORD has come, because it is near—"*

God has set His alarm clock, and it is time to reap your unclaimed riches. However, some believers are so asleep they can't even hear His alarm. Others keep hitting the snooze button because they are not quite ready to give up a life without lack.

The Lord does not ask you what time you would like your wake-up call, because when He gets ready, it is time to move.

Isaiah 60:1 proclaims:

*"Arise, shine, for your light has come, and the glory of the LORD has risen upon you."*

It is time to arise from the blurs of indistinction. It is time to resurrect out of the ashes of lack. It is time to come out of the land of bondage, pass over and go get your promised harvest.

Somewhere there is a remnant people who are positioned on the brink to hear God's reverberating alarm in the realm of the spirit. They do not want to miss their opportunity for deliverance.

## It's Time to Cross Over

Are you ready? This is your day; this is your hour! It doesn't matter if poverty, bankruptcy, debt or lack have shackled your hands to the wall and your feet to the floor. It doesn't matter how long you have been bound. The fields are white already to harvest! It is time for you to go get it!

Maybe the devil has tried to talk you out of your miracle. Now is not the time to sit still and do nothing. It's time to get up! It's time to arise, shine, for your light has come, and the glory of the Lord is risen upon you!

### PASSING OVER THE JORDAN

Israel was in the wilderness forty years. However, this day they fulfilled the word of the Lord:

*"The priests carrying the ark of the covenant of the LORD stood firmly on dry ground in the middle of the Jordan, and all Israel crossed over on dry ground until the entire people completed crossing over the Jordan"* (Joshua 3:17).

## Unclaimed Riches

Like the Israelites, it may seem as though you have been wandering in the wilderness for years. However, when your Heavenly Father bids you come, come you will, for you have heard His voice with supernatural clarity and you will cross over without hesitation or delay.

Peter hearkened unto the Lord's voice to step out of the boat though the winds were contrary and the storm was raging.

*Peter answered Him and said, "Lord, if it is You, bid me come to You on the water." He said, "Come." And when Peter got out of the boat, he walked on the water, to go to Jesus"* (Matthew 14:28-29).

We must leave the past behind and follow our Commander-in-Chief onward to our Canaan land. The Gospel of Matthew records:

*Then Jesus said to His disciples, "If anyone will come after Me, let him deny himself, and take up his cross, and follow Me.*

*For whoever would save his life will lose it, and whoever loses his life for My sake will find it"* (Matthew 16:24-25).

We are about to enter a land where we must totally depend upon the Lord for everything. Though the promised land contains our unclaimed riches, God will never create a life for us in which He is unnecessary.

When we totally depend upon Jesus, He promises us:

*"Come to Me, all you who labor and are heavily burdened, and I will give you rest"* (Matthew 11:28).

The Lord wants you to enter into your rest. Rest simply means this: don't be troubled in troubled waters!

The Lord has covered you with His presence; therefore, you have no reason to fear the terror by night nor the arrow by day. Now is the time to go and get everything that belongs to you.

## SEIZING THE WALLED CITIES

Have you seized the walled cities? Have you stared the giants of your life down in utter defiance? Our great leader and liberator, the Lord Jesus Christ, is sifting through the self-indulgent and the self-satisfied.

The previous generation was gripped with greed and fear. Forty years later, however, this generation caught a glimpse of the palm trees of Jericho just across Jordan. Then they knew in three days they would gather the fruit.

Wanderers were about to become conquerors, and they now crossed over into the land of promises.

## Five

## *Building A Memorial*

God delights in memorials. Throughout the Bible He admonished His people, "Everywhere you go, build an altar there in remembrance that I met you there."

After the Israelites crossed the Jordan River they built a memorial unto the Lord in remembrance of God bringing them into the promised land.

Joshua 4:4-7 records:

*So Joshua summoned the twelve men he had appointed from among the children of Israel, one man per tribe. Then Joshua said to them, "Cross over before the ark of the* LORD *your God into the middle of the Jordan. Each of you lift up a stone upon your shoulder, one for each of the tribes of the children of Israel, so that this will be a sign among you. When your children ask, 'What do these stones mean to you?' you will answer them that the wa-*

*ters of the Jordan were cut off before the ark of the covenant of the LORD. When it crossed the Jordan, the waters of the Jordan were cut off. These stones will be a memorial for the children of Israel continually.*

Joshua also built a memorial before the priests ascended out of the river. Twelve stones were placed one upon another. This memorial was to serve as a perpetual remembrance that Israel had been there.

*"Joshua also set twelve stones in the middle of the Jordan at the place where the feet of the priests who carried the ark of the covenant were standing. The stones are there to this day"* (4:9).

What is a memorial? The International Standard Bible Encyclopedia defines a memorial as, "a sacrificial term, that which brings the offerer into remembrance before God, or brings God into favorable remembrance with the offerer."

There are many examples of memorials given throughout the Bible.

## **A Prophet Is Born**

Hannah knew about memorials. She was one of two wives married to Elkanah. However, she was barren.

Every year Elkanah and his wives went to the tabernacle to worship God. During this time, Elkanah's second wife, Peninnah, provoked Hannah because she was barren. Therefore, she wept sorely before the Lord.

The Bible then records:

> *So she made a vow and said, "O LORD of Hosts, if You will indeed look on the affliction of Your maidservant, and remember me and not forget Your maidservant, but will give to Your maidservant a baby boy, then I will give him to the LORD all the days of his life, and no razor shall touch his head." They rose up in the morning early and worshipped before the LORD. And they returned and came to their house to Ramah. And*

*Unclaimed Riches*

*Elkanah knew Hannah his wife, and the LORD remembered her* (1 Samuel 1:11,19).

Hannah cried out to God in the tabernacle for a child. She mixed her praying with her giving. Her prayer went up as a memorial before God, and He gave her the prophet, Samuel.

Not only did she give birth to one of Israel's greatest prophets, the Lord gave her six more children!

## A MEMORIAL BRINGS ABOUT VICTORY

Jephthah, the son of Gilead, was familiar with memorials. The Bible says:

*Jephthah made a vow to the LORD, "If You will indeed give the Ammonites into my hands, then whatever comes out from the door of my house to meet me, when I return safely from the Ammonites, will surely be the LORD's, and I will offer it up as a burnt offering." So Jephthah crossed over to the Ammonites to wage war against them, and the LORD gave them into his hands.*

*When Jephthah went to his house at Mizpah, there was his daughter coming out to meet him, dancing with a tambourine. She was his only child. Other than her, he had neither son nor daughter. When he saw her, he ripped up his clothes and said, "Alas, my daughter! You have brought utter disaster to me. You are my undoing, for I have given my word to the LORD, and I cannot take it back"* (Judges 11:30-32;34-35).

Jephthah was a desperate man. His prayer before God was a matter of life and death. He reached deep within himself and found the kind of prayer that gets God's attention immediately – prayer mixed with giving, because giving is an act of faith.

Jephthah told the Lord if He would give him the victory over the Ammonites, he would give Him the first thing that came through his door. Over 40,000 of Israel's enemies were slaughtered that day, and God secured Israel's victory because of the prayer of Jephthah.

## A HOUSEHOLD IS SAVED

Cornelius, a centurion, dedicated his life to mixing his praying with his giving.

*In Caesarea there was a man named Cornelius, the centurion of a band of soldiers called the Italian Detachment, a devout man and one who feared God with all his household, who gave many alms to the people and continually prayed to God. About the ninth hour of the day he saw clearly in a vision an angel of God coming in and saying to him, "Cornelius." When he looked at him he was afraid, and said, "What is it, Lord?" He said to him, "Your prayers and your alms have come up as a memorial before God"* (Acts 10:1-4).

The Bible called him a devout man, and one who feared God. God said that his prayers and his alms had come up as a memorial before Him. Therefore, He prepared Peter to show him the way of salvation. As a result, Cornelius' entire household was saved.

## PRAYER MIXED WITH GIVING

In all of these instances, men and women wrapped their faith with their life. They mixed their praying and their giving. They targeted their seed toward their need.

God, in essence, said, "I must know where your heart is in regard to your prayer. When I see your sacrifice following that prayer, I know that where your treasure is, there your heart is also."

Memorials are central to our lives so that we will remember all that God has done for us. A memorial sets a mark upon your prayer, and you will never forget that it is Jehovah Jireh, your Provider, which has made a way through the wilderness and a river in the desert.

There are many milestones in your life as you walk with God. May God help us not to be like the lepers whom Jesus healed, who never came back and said, "Thank you for cleansing me."

The Israelites remembered that it was God alone who provided a way for them to cross over.

However, now was not the time to quit. God was just beginning to move in a miraculous way. Now it was time to possess the promised land.

## Six

## *Possessing the Land of Promise*

Once the last memorial had been built on the shore of their new homeland, the last feat the Israelites were commanded to do was to possess the land.

> *"Pass through the midst of the camp and command the people, 'Prepare food, for in three days you will cross the Jordan to go to take possession of the land that the LORD your God is giving you to possess'"* (Joshua 1:11).

The word "possess" is a war term which means to drive out and spoil the previous tenants. Israel must defeat their enemies; and, with God's help, they would be driven from the land.

However, did you ever wonder why the Lord brought the Israelites over the Jordan at the time when the snow was melting and the river was overflowing its banks?

## Unclaimed Riches

As I said earlier, the manna had ceased. Therefore, Israel would need food, clothing and shelter once they passed over into the land of Canaan.

The children of Israel were told to cross over during the time when the early harvest was ripening throughout the country. The first crop of the season was ready to be reaped. Their sustenance was waiting for them.

Suppose there had been no harvest in the fields ready for reaping? How would the children of Israel have been fed when they were across the river and the manna had ceased?

### OUT OF THE HOUSE OF BONDAGE

When the Israelites took possession of Canaan it was ready for their habitation. Cities were built; houses were furnished for their use. Wells were dug which would provide water. The vineyards were flourishing consumed, and the ground was already cultivated.

*Possessing the Land of Promise*

God was about to fulfil the promise He had made to His servant, Moses, when He first brought the children of Israel out of the land of Egypt.

*"And when the Lord your God brings you into the land which He swore to your fathers, to Abraham, Isaac, and Jacob, to give you, with great and goodly cities which you did not build, And houses full of all good things which you did not fill, and cisterns hewn out which you did not hew, and vineyards and olive trees which you did not plant, and when you eat and are full, Then beware lest you forget the Lord, Who brought you out of the land of Egypt, out of the house of bondage"* (Deuteronomy 6:10-12 Amplified).

When the Israelites left Egypt, the house of bondage, they were laden with the country's wealth. Notwithstanding, for forty long years, despite their disobedience, God performed the miraculous so that their shoes and clothes never wore out;

manna fell daily from heaven and water flowed freely from a rock.

They were supernaturally sustained by God. Nevertheless, when they possessed the promised land, they owned none of it. They could not trace their ownership through their ancestors.

They owed everything to the goodness of God, since it was God who had given them the land. We owe our possessions to God, for *"no good thing will He withhold from the one who walks uprightly"* (Psalm 84:11).

## A PROMISE BECOMES A REALITY

Joshua reminded them of the promise when it had become a reality.

*"I have given you a land for which you did not labor and cities you did not build, and you dwell in them; you eat from vine-*

*yards and olive yards you did not plant"* (Joshua 24:13 Amplified).

As stated in Deuteronomy 6:12, they were not to forget the Lord God who brought them out of the land of Egypt.

Every piece of food, provision of crops and portion of land was a reminder to the Israelites that the Lord brought them into the land of plenty from the house of bondage. Every grape was a reminder of God's provision. Every handful of grain was a token of the Lord's supply. Every well was a memorial that they would no longer drink from a rock but from the rains of heaven.

Therefore, the children of Israel were commanded to love the Lord their God with all of their heart. All Jehovah asked in return was their lives in service to and the dedication of their substance to Him.

## Dwelling in the Land of Promises

God caused Israel's adversaries to prepare a great reception for their entry into their new homeland. A grand banquet waited for them in the fields. They had possessed their promised land and now it was time to dwell there.

*"And it must be, when you come into the land which the LORD your God is giving you for an inheritance, and you possess it, and dwell in it..."* (Deuteronomy 26:1).

The children of Israel were to protect the land by physically dwelling on it and becoming long term residents. The Hebrew word for dwell in Deuteronomy 26:1 is *yashab* — which means "to settle into" or "to be secure."

It refers to the place where you homestead, marry, set up housekeeping and resist all claim jumpers. To homestead required that one prove his right of ownership of his property by sowing seed and digging wells on the land.

## Possessing the Land of Promise

The Lord not only provides provision, but protection. The Psalmist said:

*He who dwells in the shelter of the Most High shall abide under the shadow of the Almighty. I will say of the* LORD, *"He is my refuge and my fortress, my God in whom I trust." Surely He shall deliver you from the snare of the hunter and from the deadly pestilence. He shall cover you with His feathers, and under His wings you shall find protection; His faithfulness shall be your shield and wall. You shall not be afraid of the terror by night, nor of the arrow that flies by day; nor of the pestilence that pursues in darkness, nor of the destruction that strikes at noonday. A thousand may fall at your side and ten thousand at your right hand, but it shall not come near you* (91:1-7).

God will drive off those who would steal the seed from the land you possess, and protect your field from intruders. We must resist <u>all</u> claim jumpers!

*Unclaimed Riches*

God told the Israelites to mark the land with a claim to ownership by sowing seed.

When you sow your seed toward your greatest need – whether it is your marriage, your children, your finances or your health – you are telling the devil that area of your life is off limits to him.

## TREASURES WORTH POSSESSING

The Israelites, dwelling in the land of plenty, felt deeply indebted to God. How much more should you and I pay homage to Him whom gave us His only Son.

*"For God so greatly loved and dearly prized the world that He [even] gave up His only begotten (unique) Son, so that whoever believes in (trusts in, clings to, relies on) Him shall not perish (come to destruction, be lost) but have eternal (everlasting) life"* (John 3:16 Amplified).

Therefore, let us offer unto God our best offering who has bestowed upon us such unclaimed riches.

In deep humility, let us set our heart upon God as our eyes look across the Jordan River. For our Lord, in His grace and goodness, has prepared for us unclaimed riches worth possessing.

May our prayer mirror that of the old hymn which says, "On Jordan's stormy banks I stand, and cast a wishful eye. To Canaan's fair and happy land, where my possessions lie!"

## Seven

## Hidden Treasures

The Israelites successfully crossed over the Jordan River and possessed the land. Now it was time to put in the sickle and reap their harvest – their unclaimed riches.

As we saw in the last chapter, the Lord brought His people to Jordan at the time when the snow was melting in the mountains, and the river was overflowing.

The Lord said through His servant, Joshua:

*"I have given you a land for which you did not labor and cities you did not build, and you dwell in them; you eat from vineyards and olive yards you did not plant"* (Joshua 24:13 Amplified).

The harvest was coming to maturity in every field throughout the land. Their crops stood in the fields ready to be gathered. Their cities were already built. The homes were already furnished. God had already provided everything the children of Israel would need to inhabit the land.

God's chosen people were prepared to possess the land, and possess it they did. The hand of God's favor was upon them. They were called and anointed for such a time as this!

## THUS SAYS THE LORD TO HIS ANOINTED

One of the greatest barometers which distinguishes our generation in the last days is this: God has begun to pour out revelation upon revelation, truth upon truth, line upon line, precept upon precept to become the building stones for us to climb out of the dungeons of poverty and lack.

For too long the church has set on the sidelines believing that someday she will walk in the blessing of God. But I have a word for you found at the beginning of verse 1 in Isaiah chapter 45:

*"Thus says the LORD to Cyrus, His anointed..."*

## Hidden Treasures

Notice the word "anointed" in this passage of scripture. Here Isaiah is referring to the pagan king, Cyrus. One hundred fifty years before he was born, Isaiah began to prophesy about this deliverer of the Jewish people.

However, though he did not serve Jehovah, God announced, through Isaiah, that he was anointed. Why? Because the Lord was going to use him to bring His people back to their own land.

The word "anointed" actually means to be painted like a target with a fragrance that attracts the favor of God.

I want you to meditate on the fact that you are anointed, or painted, with a fragrance that attracts the favor of God.

Isaiah 45:2-3 continues:

*"I will go before you and make the crooked places straight; I will break in pieces the gates of bronze and shatter the bars of iron. And I will give you the treasures of darkness and hidden*

*riches of secret places so that you may know that I, the LORD, who calls you by your name, am the God of Israel."*

God wants you to know that your harvest is already waiting for you in the fields. It may have been covered up, but the light of His word is about to reveal those treasures of darkness and hidden riches of secret places.

The prophet, Amos, prophesied your harvest is already waiting for you when he said:

*"Indeed the days are coming, says the LORD, when the plowman will overtake the one who is reaping, and the treader of grapes the one who is sowing the seed; the mountains will drip sweet wine, and all the hills will flow with it"* (9:13).

There is coming a time in the body of Christ when the reapers are going to overtake the sowers. This means there is coming a time when you are going to put in the seed with one hand and before it can hit the ground, with the other hand you are going to reap. Faster than you can get your seed sown, you will be taking a harvest out. You are living in the time when your harvest is already in the field! God is just waiting on you to reap!

Let me share something else with you: you are not only going to reap where you sow, but you are going to reap where you didn't sow. You are going to reap in unusual places.

God is going to invade your everyday life with a harvest. He wants to prove to you that He alone is the Lord, and He will show up regardless of what you have done or what you are expecting.

That is what the anointing is about. It is the perpetual power of the energy of God which will propel you through every line of Satan's defense!

Like Joshua and the children of Israel, we are trespassing into enemy held territory, because God is going to shower us with a great downpour of blessing so that we have enough left over to help finance the Gospel to lost and hurting humanity!

## THE WEALTH OF THE WORLD

I want you to understand that at this very moment in time it is our covenant right to go get our promised harvest. The wealth the world has laid up belongs to us.

Proverbs 13:22 declares:

*"A good man leaves an inheritance to his children's children, and the wealth of the sinner is laid up for the just."*

We are going to invade enemy held territory, and all along the way God is going to drop some blessings for you to pick up. It is time to start walking around in the atmosphere of expectancy. The adversary has walked into your life and your home and stolen from you. However, we are about to take back everything he has stolen!

The Book of Proverbs says:

*"Men do not despise a thief if he steal to satisfy himself when he is hungry; But if he is found, he will restore sevenfold; he will give all the substance of his house"* (6:30-31).

## AN IMMEDIATE HARVEST

Mark 4:26-29 says:

*He said, "The kingdom of God is like a man who scatters seed on the ground. He sleeps and rises night and day, and the seed sprouts and grows; he does not know how. For the earth bears fruit by itself: first the blade, then the head, then the full seed in the head. But when the grain is ripe, immediately he applies the sickle because the harvest has come."*

The harvest cannot wait. It is the shortest period of time in the reproductive growth of your seed. You can leave your seed in your barn and it will still bring forth a harvest.

## Unclaimed Riches

Just like the Lord prepared a harvest for the Israelites, He has prepared a harvest for you. It is time to get your unclaimed riches.

We are in the season of harvest. Even if you have to work all night, when the grain fields turn golden brown you can't wait to bring in the harvest.

We have crops that have rotted in the field. We have blamed God for not answering our prayer when in reality He gave seed to the sower, and the sower sowed the seed and God gave the increase.

The seed will do what it is supposed to do. It is the nature of a seed to reproduce. It is not our responsibility to know how the seed grows. The seed and the soil will do what they are designed to do.

God will do his part. He gives the increase. You have yet to pray a prayer that He did not answer. Every seed that you have ever sown has produced a harvest, but because we have not

## *Hidden Treasures*

actively known how to reap it, our harvest has been ruined in the field.

The Lord heard your prayer, and He answered that prayer. He multiplied your seed sown.

### TIME IS SHRINKING

Genesis 8:22 says:

*"While the earth remains, seedtime and harvest, cold and heat, summer and winter, and day and night will not cease."*

We can bear witness that, according to Jehovah's covenant, seedtime and harvest, cold and heat, summer and winter and day and night have not ceased. The world is full of evidence to God's never ending faithfulness.

However, God made no mention of what goes on between seedtime and harvest. The closer we get to the imminent return of Jesus Christ of Nazareth, the shorter time will become.

*Unclaimed Riches*

I have a good friend who is a farmer. During harvest time he will have his combines out day and night, if necessary, to bring in the harvest. Why? Because this is the shortest time in the planting process. One year, they couldn't get the harvest in fast enough, so a portion of it rotted in the field.

Time is shrinking. There is not going to be any in between time. The treader of grapes is crushing the grapes under his feet, and he hasn't sown any seed yet. As quickly as the seed hits the ground, you are going to harvest it. There are a lot of things still left to do, and that is why God said he would do a quick work in these last days. Your harvest is already there!

## UNCLAIMED RICHES FOR THE LAST DAYS

Let me leave you with this final word: it was spring when the children of Israel prepared to pass over the Jordan River. It was during the time of barley harvest, when Jordan overflows all its banks and the river becomes a torrential current.

Joshua 3:15 explains it this way:

*"When the carriers of the ark came to the Jordan, the feet of the priests carrying the ark dipped into the edge of the water. (Now the Jordan overflows its banks all the days of the harvest.)"*

Why did the Lord bring His people to the Jordan when the snow was melting and overflowing the banks of the river?

The explanation is this: It was then that the harvest was ripening throughout Canaan.

What if there were no crops in the fields ready to harvest? How would the children of Israel be fed when they were across the river and the manna ceased?

Their food stood in the fields ready to be gathered. The livelihood of Israelites' enemies was about to become their supply in their newly acquired land. There was a great transfer to God's chosen people.

## Unclaimed Riches

In this final hour of human history, there's about to be a tremendous transfer of wealth to this generation.

Ecclesiastes chapter 2:26 states:

*"To the man who pleases him, God gives wisdom, knowledge and happiness, but to the sinner he gives the task of gathering and storing up wealth to hand it over to the one who pleases God" (NIV).*

James 5:1-3 begins by speaking to the world:

*"Come now, you rich men, weep and howl for your miseries that shall come upon you. Your riches are corrupted and your garments are moth-eaten. Your gold and silver are corroded, and their corrosion will be a witness against you and will eat your flesh like fire. You have stored up treasures for the last days."*

Verse 7 continues:

*"Therefore be patient, brothers, until the coming of the Lord. Notice how the farmer waits for the precious fruit of the earth and is patient with it until he receives the early and late rain."*

The Lord has strategically positioned those whom He will cause to gather large sums of wealth for the purpose of transferring it to His kingdom for the financing of the Gospel. That's why He said in verse 7, *"Be patient."*

I like to say it this way, "Hold on." Your harvest is already on the way. Your boss may not be saved, but hold on. The wealth of the wicked is laid up for the just. You may be living paycheck to paycheck, but hold on. God is about to open the windows of heaven and pour you out a blessing there is not room enough to contain.

Your harvest begins by placing a demand upon your faith. Maybe you are facing one of the greatest financial burdens of your life. John 16:33 says:

## Unclaimed Riches

*"I have told you these things so that in Me you may have peace. In the world you will have tribulation. But be of good cheer. I have overcome the world."*

Before you get your seed out of your hand, your promised harvest of unclaimed riches are already waiting for you. It is time to go get your unclaimed riches!

# *Receiving Your Unclaimed Riches*

*"And when the Lord your God brings you into the land which He swore to your fathers, to Abraham, Isaac, and Jacob, to give you, with great and goodly cities which you did not build, And houses full of all good things which you did not fill, and cisterns hewn out which you did not hew, and vineyards and olive trees which you did not plant, and when you eat and are full, Then beware lest you forget the Lord, Who brought you out of the land of Egypt, out of the house of bondage"* (Deuteronomy 6:10-12 Amplified).

*"But you must remember the LORD your God, for it is He who gives you the ability to get wealth, so that He may establish His covenant which He swore to your fathers, as it is today"* (Deuteronomy 8:18).

*"Then Joshua commanded the officers of the people, "Pass through the midst of the camp and command the people, 'Prepare food, for in three days you will cross the Jordan to go to take possession of the land that the LORD your God is giving you to possess'"* (Joshua 1:10-11).

*"I have given you a land for which you did not labor and cities you did not build, and you dwell in them; you eat from vineyards and olive yards you did not plant"* (Joshua 24:13 Amplified).

*"Praise ye the LORD. Blessed is the man who fears the LORD, who delights greatly in His commandments. His offspring shall be mighty in the land; the generation of the upright shall be blessed. Wealth and riches shall be in his house, and his righteousness endures forever"* (Psalm 112:1-3).

*"A good man leaves an inheritance to his children's children, and the wealth of the sinner is laid up for the just"* (Proverbs 13:22).

*"Through wisdom is a house built, and by understanding it is established..."* (Proverbs 24:3).

*"To the man who pleases him, God gives wisdom, knowledge and happiness, but to the sinner he gives the task of gathering and storing up wealth to hand it over to the one who pleases God"* (Ecclesiastes 2:26, NIV).

*"See, I will do a new thing, now it shall spring forth; shall you not be aware of it? I will even make a way in the wilderness, and rivers in the desert"* (Isaiah 43:19).

*"I will go before you and make the crooked places straight; I will break in pieces the gates of bronze and shatter the bars of iron. And I will*

*give you the treasures of darkness and hidden riches of secret places so that you may know that I, the LORD, who calls you by your name, am the God of Israel"* (Isaiah 45:2-3).

*"I will also save you from all your uncleanness. And I will call for the grain and increase it and lay no famine upon you. I will multiply the fruit of the tree and the increase of the field so that you shall receive no more reproach of famine among the nations"* (Ezekiel 36:29-30).

*"For I know the thought and plans that I have for you, says the Lord, thoughts and plans for welfare and peace and not for evil, to give you hope in your final outcome"* (Amplified).

*"Come, let us return to the LORD, for He has torn, and He will heal us. He has struck, and He will bind us up. After two days He will revive us. On the third day He will raise us up, that we may live before Him. Let us know, let us press on to know the LORD. His appearance is as*

*sure as the dawn. He will come to us like the rain; like the spring rains He will water the earth"* (Hosea 6:1-3).

*"Indeed the days are coming, says the* LORD, *when the plowman will overtake the one who is reaping, and the treader of grapes the one who is sowing the seed; the mountains will drip sweet wine, and all the hills will flow with it"* (Amos 9:13).

*He said, "The kingdom of God is like a man who scatters seed on the ground. He sleeps and rises night and day, and the seed sprouts and grows; he does not know how. For the earth bears fruit by itself: first the blade, then the head, then the full seed in the head. But when the grain is ripe, immediately he applies the sickle because the harvest has come"* (Mark 4:26-29).

*"That the God of our Lord Jesus Christ, the Father of glory, may give unto you the spirit of wisdom and revelation in the knowledge of him:*

*The eyes of your understanding being enlightened; that ye may know what is the hope of his calling, and what the riches of the glory of his inheritance in the saints, And what is the exceeding greatness of his power to usward who believe, according to the working of his mighty power"* (Ephesians 1:17-19).

*"But my God shall supply your every need according to His riches in glory by Christ Jesus"* (Philippians 4:19).

*"...giving thanks to the Father, who has enabled us to be partakers in the inheritance of the saints in light. He has delivered us from the power of darkness and has transferred us into the kingdom of His dear Son..."* (Colossians 1:12-13).

*"And without faith it is impossible to please God, for he who comes to God must believe that He exists and that He is a rewarder of those who diligently seek Him"* (Hebrews 11:6).

## Receiving Your Unclaimed Riches

*"Beloved, I pray that all may go well with you and that you may be in good health, even as your soul is well"* (3 John 2).

## About the Author

ROD PARSLEY is pastor of World Harvest Church in Columbus, Ohio, a dynamic megachurch that touches lives worldwide and streams 24/7 around the world on iHarv.tv. He is also a highly sought-after crusade and conference speaker who delivers a life-changing message to raise the standards of physical purity, moral integrity and spiritual intensity.

Parsley also hosts *Breakthrough*, a daily television broadcast, seen by millions across America and around the world, as well as oversees Bridge of Hope Missions Outreach, World Harvest Ministerial Alliance, Valor Christian College and Harvest Preparatory School. He is also the author of more than 50 books including the *New York Times* best-seller *Culturally Incorrect*, and his most recent, *Gone…One Man…One Tomb…One Sunday…* He and his wife, Joni, have two children, Ashton and Austin.

# CONNECT
## WITH **ROD PARSLEY**

- **RodParsley**
- **@RealRodParsley**

## iHarv.tv
*Sunday Everyday*

## 24 hour live stream of anointed messages and powerful music!

Dedicated **iPastors** are available online to pray with you and support you. Chat **LIVE** during service times, or email your needs as you watch the anointed programming on our 24/7 stream of worship and ministry from World Harvest Church.

# Have you made *heaven* your eternal home?

If not, there's no better time than right now, and a caring *Breakthrough* prayer partner is ready to minister to you in prayer when you call our toll free *Breakthrough Prayer Line*, **(888) 534-3838**. They'll also send you a copy of Dr. Rod Parsley's booklet, *New Direction* that will help you along your walk with the Lord.

For more information about *Breakthrough*,
World Harvest Church, Valor Christian College,
Harvest Preparatory School, The Center for Moral Clarity, or
to receive a product list of the many books, CDs, and DVDs
by Rod Parsley, write or call:

**BREAKTHROUGH/WORLD HARVEST CHURCH**
P.O. Box 100
Columbus, OH 43216-0100
1-800-637-2288
www.RodParsley.com

**VALOR CHRISTIAN COLLEGE**
P.O. Box 800
Columbus, OH 43216-0800
(614) 837-4088
www.ValorCollege.com

**HARVEST PREPARATORY SCHOOL**
P.O. Box 400
Canal Winchester, OH 43110-0400
(614) 382-1111
www.HarvestPrep.org

**THE CENTER FOR MORAL CLARITY**
P.O. Box 100
Columbus, OH 43216-0100
(614) 837-1990
http://CMC.RodParsley.com

If you need prayer, Breakthrough Prayer Warriors are ready
to pray with you 24 hours a day, 7 days a week at
(866) 241-4292